IMAGES
of Scotland

WISHAW

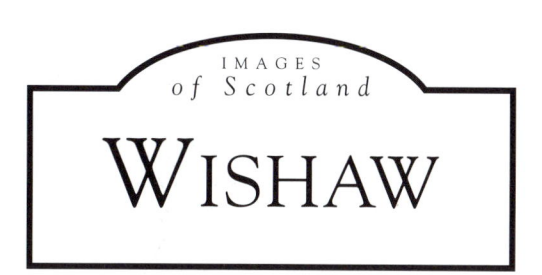

To Tom and Ann
with sincere thanks
and best wishes

Helen Moir
August 2000

The Old Castle Bar, Cleland c.1905. 'Wee Bella' is at the door.

IMAGES
of Scotland

WISHAW

Compiled by
Helen Moir

TEMPUS

First published 2000
Copyright © Helen Moir, 2000

Tempus Publishing Limited
The Mill, Brimscombe Port,
Stroud, Gloucestershire, GL5 2QG

ISBN 0 7524 1887 4

Typesetting and origination by
Tempus Publishing Limited
Printed in Great Britain by
Midway Clark Printing, Wiltshire

Nicole Tollan, aged 14 months in January 2000. My beautiful granddaughter to whom this book is dedicated.

Helen Moir, authoress. Proud grandmother of Nicole Tollan.

Contents

Acknowledgements	6
Introduction	7
1. A Walk Around Wishaw	9
2. The Big House	27
3. Transport	33
4. Haulage	37
5. Industry	43
6. Commerce	51
7. Churches	63
8. Schools	67
9. Do You Recognize Anyone?	71
10. Another Walk Around Wishaw	81

Acknowledgements

I would like to give a very special thank you to the following people and institutions: Kenny Clark, Bill Scott, Motherwell Heritage Centre (Brian Kirk and Margaret McGarry), Wishaw Library, Wishaw Academy Primary School, Mr James Chapman, Mr John McKillop, Mr and Mrs James Hunter, Mr Douglas Miller, Matt McCluckie, Mr Ian Skelly, Jim Ballantyne, Margaret Govan, Eileen Gourlay, Mrs Jessie Shaw senior and her daughter Jessie Shaw, Cllr John Pentland and the Parliamentary Office in Main Street, Mr James Allan and Mrs Grace Allan, Tom Snedden and Mr Bob Martin.

This book could not have been accomplished without their help and donations of precious material.

I would also like to give a very special thank you to Mr John McKillop of the Lanarkshire Legacy Series, Kenny Clark, Tom Snedden and Cllr John Pentland for their marvellous support and their belief in my work.

Finally, a special mention to my husband Bill for his love and support, my daughter Kirsteen Tollan and son-in-law Thomas, my son Andrew Sykes and, of course, the reason for doing the book, my granddaughter Nicole Tollan.

Introduction

The town of Wishaw lies about fifteen miles south-east of Glasgow and is situated in what was once part of the highly industrialized county of Lanarkshire. Wishaw itself lies within the ancient parish of Cambusnethan, but the history of the town that we know as Wishaw today is comparatively recent.

There are various theories as to the name of Wishaw and its origins. The word 'schaw' or shaw' is of Anglo Saxon origins and means 'a small wood'. The word 'Wi' could be a corruption of 'Via', thereby giving us ' a road through a wood'. There is another theory that it is derived from the name of an ancient inn that was on the way to St Winifred's Well. The legend goes that the inn was known by the invalids and pilgrims as the 'Wish Ha'. Whatever the origin of the name, it has been lost in the mists of time and all we can do nowadays is ponder on its origins.

Wishaw first appeared on a map in 1789 when John Ainslie mapped the area. Wishaw, like many other Scottish towns, began as a series of hamlets which slowly, but surely, grew together to form a larger conurbation. On Ainslie's map the name of Wishaw is clearly visible, as are those of Coalness, Muirhouse, Murdieston and Cleland. As well as these that of the Belhaven Inn is also noted. From these small settlements came the town of Wishaw.

While the town of Wishaw is relatively modern, the history of the area goes back to pre-Roman times. A Roman road cuts right through the area on its way from Hadrian's Wall to the outposts on the Antonine frontier to the north. This road crossed the river Calder below Wishaw House and near the old village of Coalness. Archaeological digs in the area have given us an insight into life in this frontier area at the time of the Romans

The next major upheaval in the area was the introduction of Christianity. St Nethan gave his name to Cambusnethan and there is evidence of other early saints within local place names and folklore. St Nethan himself was Welsh and was the brother of St Gwynog and was just one of a breed of roving missionaries who first brought Christianity to the area. Other local saints included St Serf (Dalserf), St Ninian and St Cadoc. Cambusnethan's name originates from the time of that first Christian missionary and its literal meaning in Gaelic is 'bend of the river of St Nethan'.

Large dwelling houses in the area are Wishaw House, Cambusnethan Priory, Coltness House and Allanton House. They all have a long and chequered history. Wishaw House was the seat and home of the Hamiltons of Belhaven. Wishaw House dates from 1665 and some parts of the house may be older. Cambusnethan Priory or House was completed by 1820 but near the site there had been a manor house. The estate belonged to the Lockhart family of Castlehill.

Coltness House was originally a manor house and belonged to the Stewarts of Allanton.

The seventeenth century was a period of great turmoil and the area saw some of its most turbulent times then. The effects of the Reformation and religous squabbles that culminated in the Covenating period affected the parish of Cambusnethan greatly. The Stewarts of Allanton were of the faith and were persecuted as a result, but the most noteworthy incident was the murder of Alexander Inglis of Netherton. The day after the Battle of Bothwell Bridge he was caught reading a bible while tilling his fields and was murdered as a result by a band of dragoons. He was buried in the graveyard at Carbarns. By the start of the eighteenth century laws had been passed and both Protestant and Catholic denominations settled down to peace.

Weaving became a staple industry in the town and many houses had a hand loom producing cloth. However, the main factor for the growth of Wishaw was coal. There were rich seams of coal and ironstone in the area. The discovery of coal transformed the area both above and below ground. Collieries were built and people flooded into the area to work in them. They included Berryhill and Heathery, Thornlie, Belhaven, Wishaw, Garriongill and Herdshill. Wishaw ELL coal was famous the world over. As well as coal, iron was also King in the area and there were many iron and steel works. With the coming of the Wishaw & Coltness Railway in 1839, it was easier to transport the goods of the area to world markets.

Henry Houldsworth, owner of the Coltness estate was a major force in the industrialization of the area and was responsible for the founding of the Coltness Iron Company and the opening of its first blast furnaces. Years later, David Colville also saw an opportunity to exploit the mineral resources of the area and built some of the largest steel works in Britain. Other names of long-gone firms included the Excelsior Works, Etna Iron & Steel Co., and the Glasgow Iron Co. They are all long gone.

In 1950 the passing of the Iron and Steel Act led to the construction of Ravenscraig at Craigneuk. On 2 August 1957 the blast furnaces were lit for the first time. The 'Craig had a chequered history, but its furnaces were extinguished by a political decision made by the Thatcher Government. On 27 June 1992, 1,220 men were made redundant. There are still iron and steel founders in the town, but nothing on the scale of Ravenscraig. The towers that once dominated the Lanarkshire skyline have gone. The site has been cleared and, apart from memories, little remains to suggest there was once a huge works here covering many acres.

After this major setback to employment in the area, Wishaw has bounced back and has become, once more, a thriving town. There are lots of amenities for local people and the delights of Strathclyde Country Park are a short distance away. After years of decline, the town is on the way back up again.

One
A Walk Around Wishaw

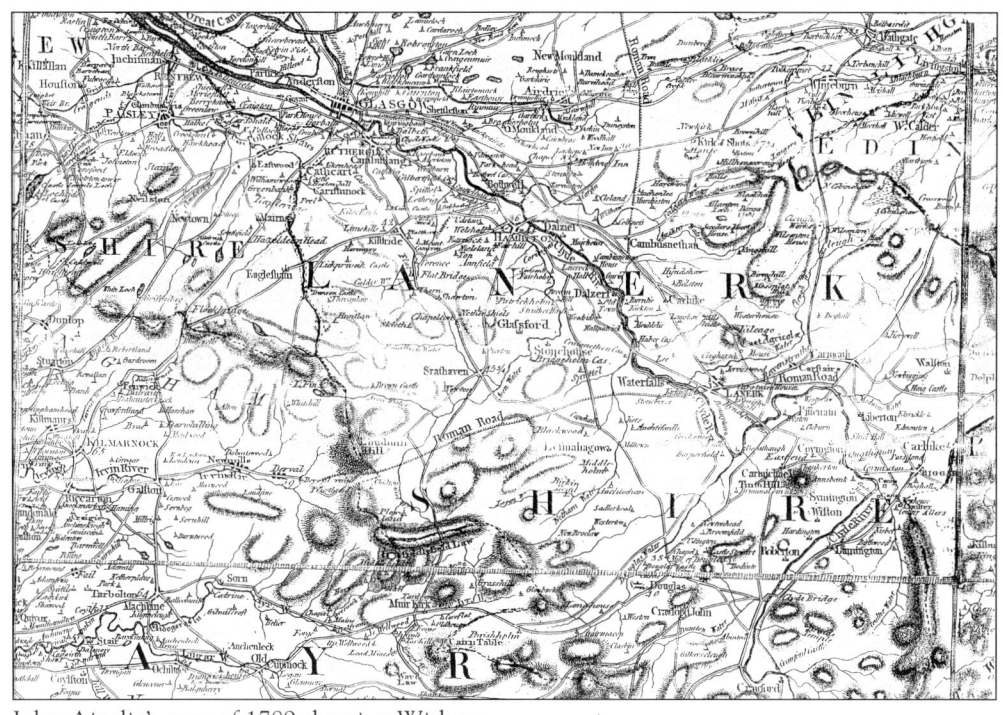

John Ainslie's map of 1789 showing Wishaw.

Main Street, Wishaw, sometime in the 1940s or 1950s. Cars were not very common at this time as most new models were exported.

Stewarton Street looking west, c.1950s. The old Bush Pit was a short distance from the end of the street and employed some of the men and boys living here. The pit belonged to the Coltness estate.

Kirk Road sometime in the 1930s with a motor bus in view. There had been a rapid expansion of bus services in the years after the First World War, which culminated in the decline of the Tramways.

Caledonian Road, shown here, was named after the Caledonian Railway Company which came to Wishaw in the late 1840s. Caledonian Road is much changed today and is unrecognisable from this tranquil scene of yesteryear.

The unusually named Cockethat, Wishaw.

The West Cross, Wishaw, before the First World War. The Cross was always an area where men would hang out, especially during the horrendous pit strikes of 1911 and 1912 and the great strike of 1926.

Manse Road, Netherton. The name of Netherton means 'low lying farmstead' – the nether town – and it was situated on the Cambusnethan estate.

Although the Wishaw area was heavily industrialized, rural amenities were close at hand. Many a picnic or a swim could be had here at the River Calder.

13

The bandstand in Belhaven Park reminds me of a Roman or Greek arena. Wishaw had a number of excellent bands. Most were works bands and they included the Coltness Iron Works Band, the Wishaw Band and the Wishaw Orchestra. The bands were supported by the owners as they generated a certain amount of rivalry between the different works and, as Henry Houldsworth of the Coltness Iron Works thought, being creative in a band was better than sitting drinking in the pub!

Russell Street was where the main Co-op was situated and was the assembly point for the Co-op Gala Day. This scene shows the 1912 Gala when over 3,000 children would have been standing in the street before being marched off behind local bands to organized events in a nearby field. Treats would have included a bag with a sandwich, cake and biscuit and entertainment would have included sports and other games.

Coltness Mill and Bridge at the turn of the last century.

A view of the River Clyde near to the Garrion Bridge. The bridge crosses the Clyde linking the two ancient parishes of Dalserf and Cambusnethan.

15

Waterloo was named after the famous battle. Sir James Stewart of the Coltness estate was present at this great victory over Napoleon and was actually the oldest officer in the British army at the time.

Another view of Waterloo from about 1905.

This much more recent image was taken by John McKillop, compiler of the Lanarkshire Legacy series, and shows a much altered view of West Cross. The Cross was once known as the 'Fit o' the Toun'.

Stewarton Street looking along towards Main Street, again on a view by John McKillop.

This particular crossroads marks the confluence of Main Street, Low Main Street, Glen Road, Glasgow Road, Belhaven Road and Marshall Street.

The era is the early 1950s and the view is of East Cross and Kirk Road. Note the total lack of congestion on the road.

A 1920s view of East Cross showing the tram lines. They belonged to the Hamilton, Motherwell & Wishaw Tramway Co. The trams started running in 1903 and ceased running less than thirty years later. Just as a point of interest, trams were introduced into the United Kingdom in the middle of the nineteenth century in Birkenhead by an American engineer called Mr Train.

Kenilworth Avenue c.1930s.

A First World War period view of Overtown. The name Overtown means 'high farmstead'.

Jacob's Ladder, near Overtown, was a popular site for locals who would often take day trips out here. It was named after the biblical Jacob. James Glidden of Overtown, the aothor's brother-in-law, remembers taking walks here as a young boy

20

Low Main Street during the early years of the twentieth century. At this time photographers were an unusual sight and could attract a large crowd such as the one shown here.

Low Main Street again. With a total lack of traffic it was possible for people to have a chat in the middle of the street.

Caledonian Road, c.1905.

West Thornlie Street, c.1905. Thornlie Church steeple is on the left.

Wishaw Main Street, c.1955. This was the real era of the cinema and lovely Art Deco buildings like this one were a common sight in main streets of Scotland.

Belhaven Park bandstand sometime in the 1930s.

Shieldmuir Road, c.1905. The Excelsior Iron Works was established here in 1866 by John William & Co. The company brought experienced workers from the Midlands to work at the iron works. English Row was built to house the influx of workers.

Glasgow Road, Wishaw, in the 1920s. The works on the right is the Clydesdale Distilley, which was owned by Lord Belhaven. He also owned a number of pits in the area, namely the Quarry Pit and the Distillery Pit.

The Fit o' the Toun at the turn of the last century.

Kirk Road at the turn of the last century. This photo dates from after 1903 because it shows the tram lines.

1930s Wishaw. How peaceful it is compared with Wishaw today

The corner of Graham Street and Stewarton Street on a view in the Lanarkshire Legacy Series by John McKillop. The shop on the corner was at one time called 'Deaf Meg's Shop'.

Two
The Big House

Wishaw House was the home and seat of Lord Belhaven and Stenton. The Lord at the time was Alexander James Hamilton. He joined the army and had a distinguished career, fighting in the Zulu War of 1879 and commanding the Surrey Brigade of Rifle Volunteers for thirteen years.

The central part of Wishaw House was said to date from 1665, but some parts are considerably older. In the nineteenth century it was expanded under the direction of Mr Gillespie Graham to take the form shown here.

Alexander James Hamilton, Lord Belhaven and Stenton. Lord Belhaven married Georgina Katharine in 1880. She was a noted member of the Societies for Prevention of Cruelty to Children and Animals and did much admirable work in improving the conditions of pit ponies working on the estate.

The sad remains of this once glorious mansion in a recent view by John McKillop. It is always a shame to see once great houses turned into ruins by years of neglect.

Coltness House, c.1916. The house and estate originally belonged to the Stewart family and the land was purchased by Sir Walter Stewart of Allanton for his younger brother, James, in 1653. The house was purchased by the Houldsworth family in 1836.

Another view of Coltness House.

The Houldsworth family owned the house until 1952 when it was sold to Dr Barnado's. It was used until 1978 as a residential home and school.

Cambusnethan House was built in the year 1820 to replace an earlier house which had been destroyed by fire. Designed by Mr Gillespie Graham, the house was a fine specimen of Gothic architecture

Now a ruin, Cambusnethan House was the seat of the Lockharts, a notable local family.

Sir Graeme Alexander Sinclair Lockhart, Bart, was born in the same year the house was erected. He was prominent in both local and international affairs. Sir Graeme followed a military career and took part in the Persian War of 1847 as well as the Indian Mutiny of the same year. He ultimately rose to command the Seaforth Highlanders and, upon his retirement, became engrossed in local affairs.

Three
Transport

Main Street, Wishaw, *c.*1910. Trams ran in Wishaw for the last time in 1931 and were referred to locally as 'the Shooglies'.

Main Street again, taken during the First World War.

Another view of Main Street with the only motor traffic being the horse and cart and the tram. Horses were an environmentally friendly mode of transport. Even the pollution they caused was often removed and used as fertilizer on local gardens.

Stewarton Street, c.1910. The condition of the roads was always a great problem in the early years of last century. They were quite often poorly made and often muddy in winter. The part that the trams ran in was looked after by the tramway company and was often in better condition than the rest of the road.

A quiet scene in 1903. When the trams first came to town they were such a novelty that tens of thousands of people travelled on them in the first month. Less than thirty years later they had been superceded by motor buses.

35

The Old Tramcar at Dalserf. This was an ex-Glasgow horse-drawn tramcar that had been recycled to become a tearoom.

An industrial steam locomotive at the Excelsior Iron Works. From the 1850s onwards, steam locomotives of this style were a common sight at many local works. Indeed, companies like Bairds of Gartsherrie had steam locomotives that would often travel miles from the works over normal railway lines.

Four
Haulage

A lorry belonging to James Hunter & Sons. They were well known within Wishaw and the surrounding area. This view dates from about 1962.

Another truck belonging to James Hunter & Sons being loaded at Mossend Engineering.

The company was founded by James Hunter in 1886 and this view shows another of their vehicles.

This late 1950s view shows a James Hunter & Sons truck being loaded up at the Motherwell Bridge Engineering Company in Motherwell.

Do you remember Battleaxe toffee? This horse and delivery vehicle belonged to the Archibald family who owned the Battleaxe factory and produced the wonderful toffee made there.

39

This view shows one of the earliest motor vehicles owned by the Archibald family. It was used to deliver the factory's goodies throughout the area. Early delivery vans were uncomfortable and slow, being restricted to about 12mph and having solid rubber tyres. It wasn't until the 1920s that pneumatic tyres became common on vans and trucks. The Battleaxe business was founded by Mr H. Archibald.

A horse and cart belonging to the Archibald family.

A 1915 photo from the Archibald family collection. The gentleman in the photo is Jim and the horse was called 'Wee Jimmy'.

Wishaw Goods and Mineral Station on an image taken by John McKillop. In a mining area, the goods and mineral station was often busier than the passenger station. Not only was coal being exported but iron ore was being brought in to keep the steel works going and the finished steel exported throughout the world.

Years later and the Goods Station has declined considerably. The mineral railways in the area shared the same fate as many of the works they once served and have been closed. Now most goods are transported by road.

Although this photograph was taken in Thistle Street in Motherwell, the lorries of William Struthers Moir regularly delivered goods in and out of Wishaw, including to the Co-op. This firm was founded by my husband's father.

Five
Industry

A view of one of the landmarks of Wishaw, Motherwell and district that has now gone.

Costain's, at Newmains, make pre-stressed and reinforced concrete items for the construction industry. This view is by John McKillop and the factory is on the site of the old Coltness Iron Works.

Pickering & Co. is another famous Wishaw company. Photograph by John McKillop.

The above view is a typical Lanarkshire steel mill, c.1904, and gives an idea of the heavy industry that once populated this neck of Lanarkshire. This is a fifty-ton tapping furnace in operation. The pig iron is loaded in to the furnace. After being melted, the metal is allowed to flow out into ingot moulds. The metal is conveyed still hot to a Cogging Mill.

At the Cogging Mill it is rolled and cropped into large slabs of steel. From here it is taken to a Plate Mill, as shown here, and is rolled continuously until it the required thickness for the job intended. After rolling it is cut up with huge shears into the various sizes required.

This is a view of Dalziell Works.

The cooling towers of Ravenscraig in a photograph by John McKillop. Ravenscraig once employed thousands of men from the Wishaw area, but now all has gone.

On 27 June 1992 the final 1,220 men left Ravenscraig for the very last time. The closure had a devastating effect on many local businesses that relied either directly or indirectly on the steelworks.

Some of the staff of the Etna Iron & Steel Company in 1923.

This was the site of the Clyde Alloy Steel Works and is now the home of Ian Skelly's motorstore.

Matt McCluckie, of Ashgill, is the second man on the left in this view of the inside of the Clyde Alloy Works. The white strips in view are burning hot strips of steel.

Two miners descend in a cage. The man on the left has lost part of his leg, probably in an underground accident.

A view in a local colliery, complete with pit ponies. This view gives an idea of the horrendous conditions that many men had to work in.

Six
Commerce

Local businessman Ian Skelly has built up a huge garage at Craigneuk. This recent view gives an idea of the scale of the garage.

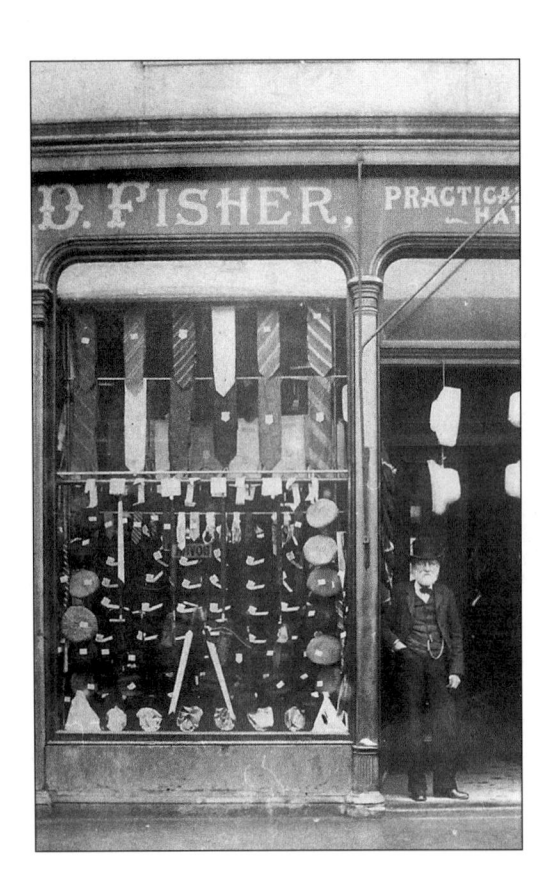

An 1890s view of the premises of Mr D. Fisher, Hatter, of Main Street, Wishaw.

This recent view by John McKillop is of Wilsons' Kirk Road.

Jean's Place, Main Street, Wishaw, by John McKillop.

Wishaw Co-op Society's shop in Russell Street, *c.*1894.

This late 1970s view of the Co-operative building in Hill Street was taken by John McKillop. The modern shop front on the ground floor very much takes away from the character of the building.

Some employees of Chapman's.

James Chapman Senior kindly supplied me with these images of his family firm. This one shows James Chapman. His wife, Mary, hailed from Carluke, where her father was a well known businessman who was also in the butcher trade. James died in 1901, but Mary continued the business until her death in 1944.

Following page: This is a view of the Chapman family taken in the late nineteenth century. Here is James Chapman, founder of the family business, with his wife, Mary Hamilton. The business has been thriving for over a hundred years.

JAS CHAPMAN

SUCCESSOR TO THE

BUTCHER.

The corner of Russell Street and Main Street, taken by John McKillop.

This firm, nicknamed the 'knicker factory', was officially known as the Clydesdale Clothing Factory and was founded by Henry Spiers. The bulk of the workforce were women and they mainly hailed from the local area.

The Clydesdale Clothing Factory was reputed to be haunted by the ghost of one of its workers.

This was once the site of Mckay & Jardine's car dealership and is now the site of the new Tesco superstore. I wish petrol was still this price!

McDonald's in Wishaw. The company have restaurants in almost every British town. The only town in the UK with a population of more than 40,000 that does not have a McDonald's is Stroud, home town of the publishers of this book.

The Commercial Hotel at the corner of Glen Road and Main Street.

The Old Customs & Excise office in Wishaw.

The bar is situated in Caledonian Road and has been refurbished since this view was taken in around 1980 by Jim Ballantyne.

This is the Barr's factory at the corner of Stewarton Street and Greenhead Road.

Frew's Garage in Craigneuk.

Seven
Churches

Thornlie Church in Caledonian Road, c.1915.

Wishaw Old Parish Church, *c.*1920.

Wishaw Old Parish Church Sunday School Walk in 1913.

St Patrick's Chapel, c.1905.

Cambusnethan church, c.1905. The name Cambusnethan is associated with St Nethan.

Cambusnethan United Free Church, c.1906.

The old graveyard at Cambusnethan.

Eight
Schools

Wishaw Academy Primary. The school was completed in 1870.

Mr Joseph Ingram, headmaster of Wishaw Public School. He was appointed headmaster of Wishaw Academy in 1873. In 1877 he was appointed as headmaster of the Public School. It had 1,300 pupils and a commensurate number of staff.

Wishaw Public School in 1904.

Wishaw Academy Primary, East Academy Street. The school was founded by the Revd P.G. Miller of Cambusnethan United Free Church and was built on land belonging to him. The school was built to serve the parishioners and to replace the Coltness Colliery School, which was located at Simpson Square, Stewarton Street.

A slate pencil sharpener from around 1870.

A view of what was once the board room of Wishaw Academy Primary School as it would have been in 1895.

An old school timetable from Wishaw Academy.

70

Nine
Do You Recognize Anyone?

Former staff of Wishaw Academy in the 1920s.

A c.1911 picture of the staff of the Battleaxe factory. Most of the workers were local women.

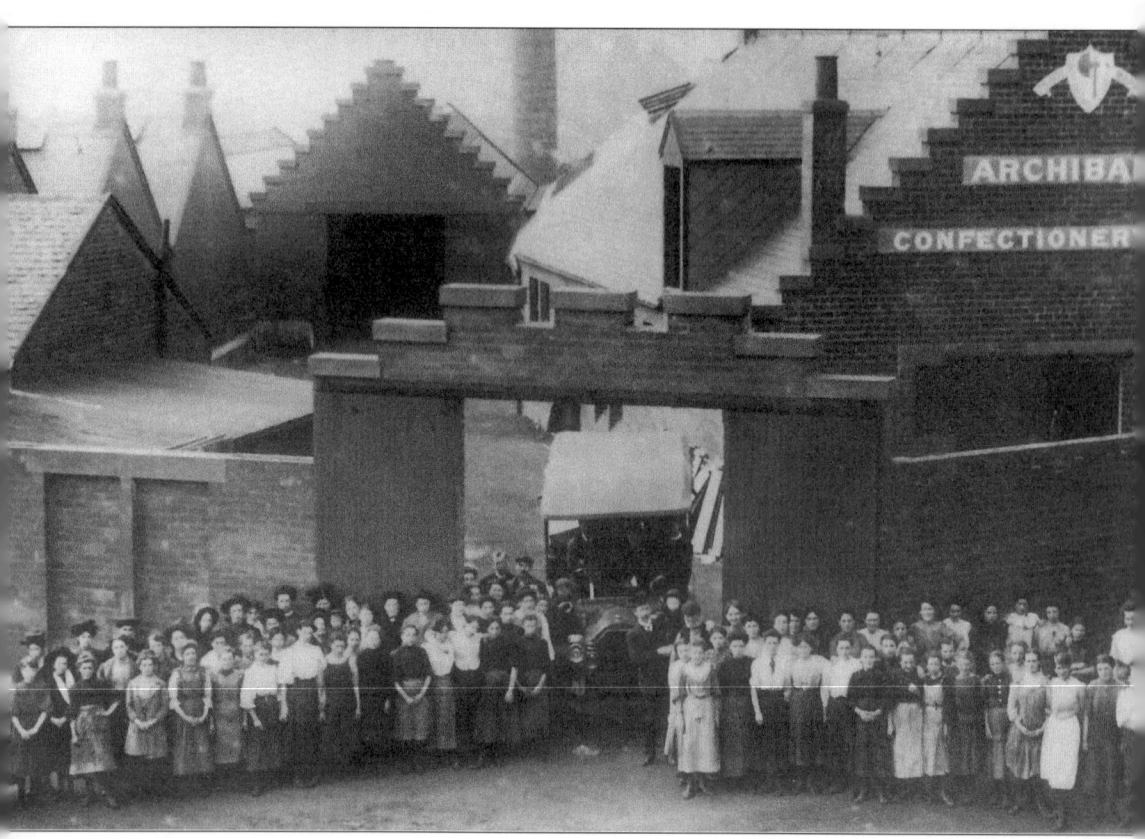

Standing outside the works are the staff of Battleaxe in the 1930s.

The staff of Battleaxe at Lanark. They visited here to see Alan Cobham's National Aviation Day. Alan Cobham travelled the country in the late 1920s and early 1930s with a flying circus to promote the use of aviation and air travel. He was forever coming up with schemes to promote air travel and was responsible for the original plans of many airfields. Over 1 million people saw his aviation days.

The Jam Section of the Battleaxe Factory, c.1940.

73

Ex-Provost Henry Archibald, the founder of Battleaxe. He was appointed provost of the unified burghs of Motherwell and Wishaw in 1920.

An outing to Lees Wood by the staff of the Glasgow Iron & Steel Company, *c.*1920.

The staff of the Glasgow Iron & Steel Company at Lees Wood in 1926.

The baker's shop at 14 Stewarton Street. This photograph was loaned to me by Eileen Gourlay who ran a successful dancing school in the town for many years. This was her aunt's shop.

75

The Old Templar's Hall, Craigneuk, c.1920s. Fourth from the left in the second row is Sarah MacAusland. Her mother, Agnes, and niece Lilly Baird are next to her.

A 1900 view of the staff at Wishaw Academy Primary School.

1940s school photographs given to me by Mr and Mrs James Hunter of James Hunter & Sons. Do you recognise anyone?

Class P4B, June 1959, Wishaw Academy Primary School. From left to right, front row: Baxter McIvor, Derek Ryder, David Sneddon, Robert Henry, John Armit. Second row: Florence Mullen, Christine Inglis, Sheila Doud, Joanne Wight, Sheena Scott, Marion Parker, Rita McCormack, Marion Hamilton. Third Row: George Lees, Graham Craik, Myra McCumisky, Hazel Mundell, Anna Morris, Christine, Young, John Murphy, James Young. Back row: Tom Dickson, Peter Millar, George Parker, Robert Hutton, Robert Watson, Malcolm Currie.

Class P3A, 1962, Wishaw Academy Primary School. From left to right, Back Row: James Jarvie, John Watson, Tom Semple, Willliam Chapman, Billy Cleland, Jan Smillie, Christopher Magnus, William Cummings. Second row: Elaine Bryson, Elizabeth Sneddon, Irene Bruce, Louisa McCully, Myra Hepburn, Janet Nelson, Christine McGonigle. Third row: Tom Sorbie, William Gray, Andrew McLeary, John Broughton (Fairground), Brian Shute, Raymond Sneddon. Front row: Robert Sneddon, Wilson Harkin, Drew Sim, Christine Ramage, Mary Lees, Ann Moore, Margaret Edment, Gail Broadhurst, David Scott, Bobby Dickson, Tom Cuthbertson.

The Staff at Wishaw Academy Primary School, March 1965. From left to right, back row: Mary Moore, Mary MacDonald, Margaret McLeod, Miss Gibson, Betty Mulholland, Janice Yule, Mrs Marshall (secretary), Mrs Wilson, Mrs Lumsden. Front row: Mrs Gowans, Betty Smith, Mrs Chambers, Mrs Watson, Mathew Barrie (Headmaster), Mr E. Loudon (First Assistant), Jean Lindsay, Mrs Joe Parton.

Wishaw Academy Primary School, 5 December 1992. The school organized a Victorian Fayre to celebrate its 125th anniversary. The event was a great success and was thoroughly enjoyed by staff, pupils and families alike.

Left: Ian Skelly, of Skelly's Garages. Both Ian and his father have been well-respected businessmen in the town for years.

Left: Councillor John Pentland, personal assistant to Frank Roy MP, has been of great assistance in the compilation of this book. He has held Ward 15 (Garrion) since 1992. Brought up in Wishaw, he has always been proud of his roots and was very active in the Trade Union movement as a shop steward at Butter Bros. It was this that brought him into politics.

Right: Frank Roy, Wishaw's MP, and Councillor John Pentland.

Ten
Another Walk Around Wishaw

The Burgh Chambers, Main Street, Wishaw, c.1910.

The 'Heathery', or to give it its posh name, Wishawhill roundabout.

Young Street and the corner of King Street. The bell tower of the original Chalmers Church is on the right with St Ignatius in the background. Again this is the the work of John McKillop, who has charted the changes in Wishaw over the years.

Quarry Street, the site of the old gas works.

The old Wishaw baths on Auchenstewart Street.

Another John McKillop photograph of the building of the new sports centre in Alexander Street.

Miner's rows were once located at this spot. This is the corner of Marshall Street and Quarry Street.

The flats at Millburn Road. The residents here could get a free look at the dog racing track.

The corner of Marshall Street and Belhaven Road. McNamee Auctioneers are situated close to the Commercial Hotel.

Part of the old gasworks looking through to Jean's Place on Main Street. A John McKillop view.

The Golden Lounge in Russell Street was once the old Co-op building. Photograph by John McKillop.

Waterloo at the turn of the twentieth century.

Overtown sometime at the beginning of the twentieth century. Much has changed here in the last hundred years.

Main Street at Jean's Place in a view taken by John McKillop.

The old Customs & Excise office. Wishaw

Main Street at the turn of the twentieth century.

Road Hill Street in recent years.

The bottom of Hill Street, adjacent to Wishaw Station.

The new Wishaw Hospital being constructed.

Charles Reid was a well known local photographer. His work was used both nationally and internationally on postcards, photographs and in newspapers and books of the day. The quality of his work, especially his nature studies, was second to none.

PHOTOGRAPHY.

Charles Reid,

YOUNG STREET, WISHAW,

BEGS to intimate that he is prepared to execute PHOTOGRAPHS in all the Popular Styles, from Carte Size upwards.

Groups, Buildings, Animals, etc.,

At a Distance, by Appointment.

To avoid disappointment, the early part of the day should be chosen for Sitting, when convenient, especially in winter.

ENLARGED PHOTOGRAPHS IN CARBON, BROMIDE, OPAL, &c.,

Copies Made from Glass Pictures, Carte, and Other Photographs.

Picture Frames in Great Variety.

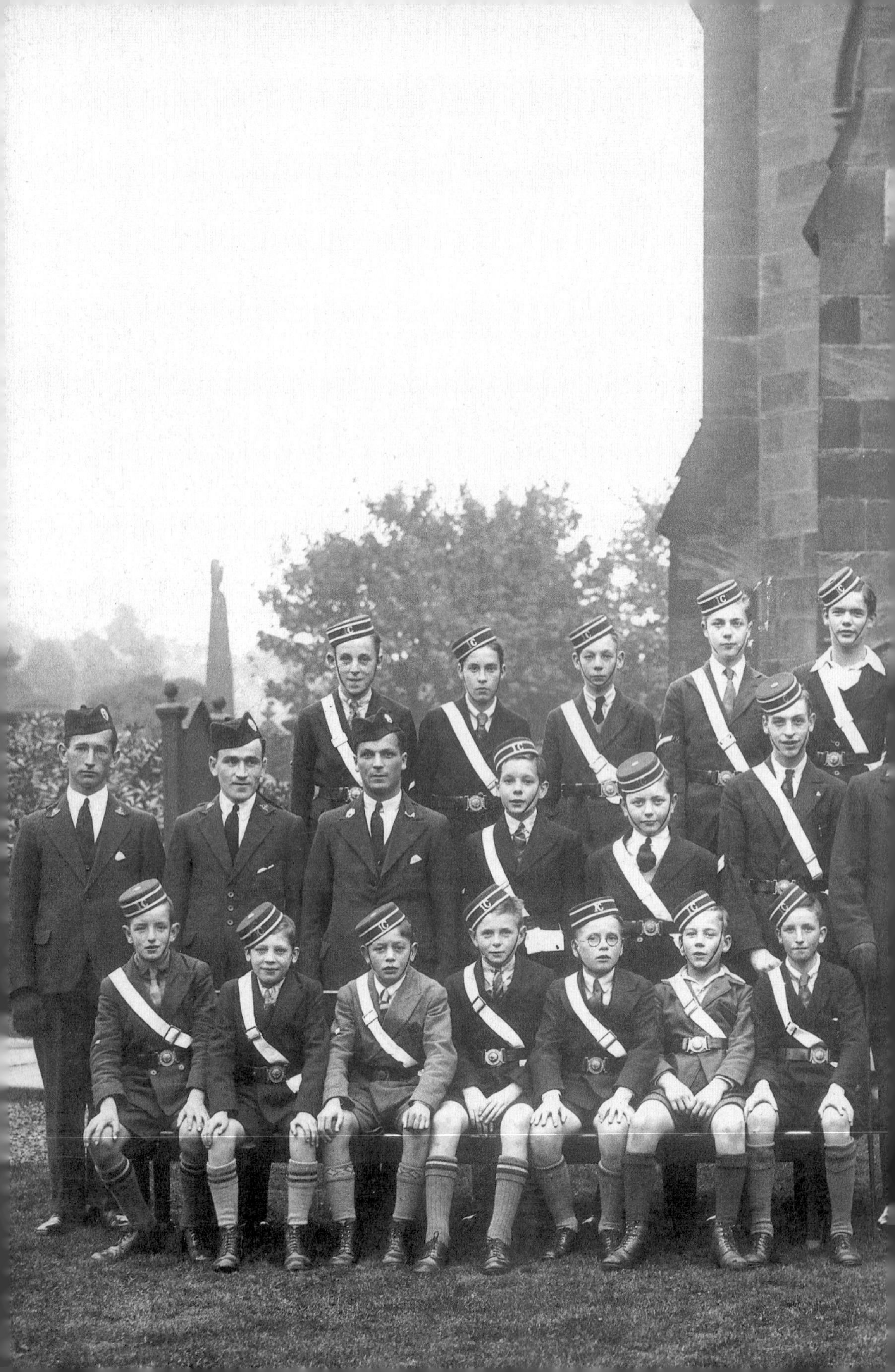

Thomas R. Lambie's

HAT, CAP, & HOSIERY WAREHOUSE,

31 Main Street, Wishaw.

HATS. CAPS. UMBRELLAS.
SCARFS. BRACES. COLLARS.
GENT.'S UNDERCLOTHING, SHIRTS, &c.

Always on hand a large Stock of above goods, which for variety, style, quality, and price, cannot be excelled at any other Establishment in town.

Umbrellas!
Umbrellas!
Umbrellas!

All kinds of Special Umbrellas Made, Re-covered, and Repaired on the shortest notice on the Premises.

—OBSERVE ADDRESS—

LAMBIE'S, 31 Main St., Wishaw.

(N.B.—Established a Quarter of a Century.)

"A MAN'S A MAN FOR A' THAT."

Whiskies from the best Distillers, either blended or not, as desired

Whiskies, Brandies, Wines, &c., of superior quality, at our usual Low Prices.

BURNS TAVERN,

MAIN STREET, WISHAW.

JOHN SMITH,

Proprietor of the above Tavern, respectfully returns thanks to his numerous Customers for past favours, and assures them that no exertions will be awanting on his part to supply Liquors of the Finest Quality, and at the most reasonable terms.

Adverts from local businesses.

CYCLES.   CYCLES.

A Well-Selected Stock of Newest and Best Patterns at Lowest Prices.

Any Kind of Tyres Fitted as desired.

Large Stock of Bells, Lamps, and Cycle Sundries.

Machines Exchanged and Repaired at Lowest Prices.

ADDRESS—

SMITH & CO.,

IRONMONGERS & CYCLE AGENTS,

49 MAIN STREET,

WISHAW.

BELLVIEW SAW MILLS,

WISHAW.

JOHN THOMSON,

WOOD MERCHANT,

JOINER, and CARPENTER.

JOINER'S SHOP—

69 STEWARTON STREET, WISHAW.

FUNERAL UNDERTAKING

IN ALL ITS DEPARTMENTS.

HEARSES, MOURNING COACHES, and every other Requisite, supplied on the Shortest Notice.

Charges strictly moderate.

Previous page: 1st Cambusnethan Boys Brigade in 1933. Bob Martin, who donated this picture, is in the back row, fourth from the left.

An advert for Eileen Gourlay, who ran a dancing school in Wishaw.

THE BALLROOM

EILEEN GOURLAY
A.I.S.T.D. (S.B.), S.D.T.A.
TEACHER OF DANCING

Private Lessons given by appointment for Ballroom and all classes of Dancing

Adult Classes in Ballroom and Tap

Juvenile Classes in Operatic, Acrobatic, Tap and Musical Comedy

For Full Particulars
WRITE, CALL OR PHONE:
THE STUDIO
200 MAIN STREET
WISHAW
LANARKSHIRE
PHONE 118

THE LOUNGE

The garrion bridge on a quiet day. There are few of those here now as this is a busy intersection of three major routes.

95

A pair of Charles Reid photographs, donated by Bob Martin. The picture above shows his father, Thomas Martin, at Wemyeshill Orchard in 1912, while the picture below is of his grandfather, Robert Martin, around the same time. The family owned Wemyeshill Orchard for over one hundred years. The tranquil ploughing scenes shown here are a stark contrast to the noise and bustle of industrial Wishaw.